How to Be an Acrobat

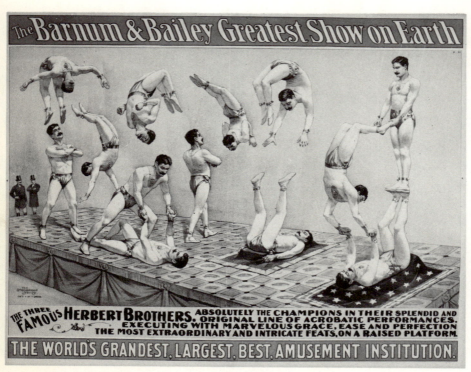

Circus World Museum, Baraboo, Wisconsin

A Ringling Bros. and Barnum & Bailey Book

HOW TO BE AN ACROBAT

Charles R. Meyer

DAVID McKAY COMPANY, INC.
NEW YORK

Library of Congress Cataloging in Publication Data

Meyer, Charles Robert, 1926-
How to be an acrobat.

(A Ringling Bros. and Barnum & Bailey book)
SUMMARY: A guide to the fundamentals of gymnastics
and acrobatics, explaining how to make them seem easy
and how to use such expertise in various
perfoming fields.
1. Acrobats and acrobatism—Juvenile literature.
[1. Acrobats and acrobatics] I. Title.
GV551.M49   796.4'7   77-4529
ISBN 0-679-20409-1

10 9 8 7 6 5 4 3 2 1

MANUFACTURED IN THE UNITED STATES OF AMERICA

To all the Ringling Bros. and Barnum & Bailey
Circus acrobats, past, present, and future,
who really wrote this book by proxy.

A Circus Prayer

O Heavenly Father, in all our circus flying, casting, whirling and twirling, allow us to share the confidence of David, the strength of Samson, the agility of Jacob, the coordination of Joseph, the dexterity of Solomon, the cooperation of Moses, the timing of Joshua and the grace of Judith.

After the grease paint has been put on, the band strikes up and the spotlights beam, let us become "all things to all men," as we show them a little bit of happiness in these troubled times. And, if You will be our special guest at every performance, in playing directly to You we will always be assured of the best of a "good audience."

Amen.

Contents

Preface

WHEN A SPACE explorer was asked by a group of Ringling Bros. and Barnum & Bailey Circus acrobats to join in their act as a joke, the astronaut answered quite seriously, "Oh, no! Your work is far too dangerous!"

Astronauts have complex electronic equipment and monitoring devices built into their vessels, and they wear life-sustaining suits when they walk on the moon. By comparison, circus acrobats must rely exclusively on their skills to keep them aloft. Each circus performer—from the clown to the aerialist—must depend on his or her own well-trained body. Each must react to the split-second decisions of his or her equally well-trained mind.

After the show is over in the Big Top, after the elephants have been watered and the ringside lights have been dimmed, circus people tell the story of the newspaper reporter who asked a famous trapeze artist

Aerialist circus acrobats, The Pendakovis. *Ringling Bros. and Barnum & Bailey Circus*

Opposite: The Flying Farfans perform triple-and-a-half somersaults. *Ringling Bros. and Barnum & Bailey Circus*

about the secret of doing a triple somersault from a swinging bar 80 feet above the net. "It is really quite simple," the trapeze performer answered. "Just keep turning, and make sure you don't pause between somersaults!"

This is excellent advice for a beginner. Acrobatics are coordinated skills used by many circus performers other than acrobats. Perhaps you want to learn to do a balancing or a "Wild West" cowboy act. Whether you're dancing, riding bareback on a horse, working with trained dogs, juggling, clowning, tightrope walking, weight-lifting or spinning around the ring as a trick cyclist, keep the trapeze artist's words in mind: "Just keep turning and make sure that you don't pause between somersaults!"

Safety is the single most important factor in training to be a circus acrobat. Here is a list of general safety precautions you should observe when you're learning the basic skills:

- Inspect your equipment regularly,
- Provide enough mats or mattresses for adequate padding so you don't take a spill on hard ground or flooring.
- Emphasize "spotting" (the buddy system of one acrobat watching another in practice sessions in order to help avoid accidents).
- Don't indulge in horseplay or roughhouse antics.
- Keep unnecessary personal gear and equipment out of all training areas.

- Allow ample time for warm-up exercises and body conditioning.
- Practice falling and landing techniques used in normal acrobatics, as well as in unexpected tumbles and spills.

Keep these simple rules in mind when you're practicing or performing before an audience. When you're "kicking sawdust" (following the circus or being part of it), you'll be a real "kinker" (veteran acrobat) instead of a "first of May" (a beginner in his or her first season with the show). Once you really get involved in this fascinating field of acrobatics and gymnastics, may you have good luck, and good spotting. And may all your performances be great ones!

1
Pre-Workout Conditioning

BASEBALL PITCHERS WARM up on the mound before a game. Runners, swimmers, prize fighters, ballet dancers, and circus acrobats go through pre-workout conditionings, too. Conditioning and warm-ups prepare circus performers for the strenuous demands made on them during gymnastic and acrobatic routines.

Start slowly on your first day, then gradually increase the pace and length of time of your warm-up exercises. If things seem hard in the beginning, don't be discouraged. You'll be learning coordination and what the experts call "motor ability," as you progress and continue to practice.

Opposite: Bridget Ballantine demonstrates a conditioning and warm-up exercise. *Ringling Bros. and Barnum & Bailey Circus*

To start your workout, stand erect, with your hands on your hips and your feet about one foot to 18 inches apart. Hold your head high. This will always be your starting position. Rotate your head to the left in a circular pattern, counterclockwise, ten to twelve times. Next, repeat the identical exercise, but this time rotate your head to the right, clockwise. If at any time you feel yourself getting dizzy or developing a headache, stop immediately and wait until the next day before you continue the exercises.

Go back to the original starting position, standing with your hands on your hips and your feet about one foot to 18 inches apart. Now, stretch out your arms full length. Your arms should be level with your shoulders, as if you had wings. Circle your arms forward, just as you rotated your head in the previous exercise. Then rotate your arms backward. Repeat this exercise ten or twelve times in each direction.

Take the starting position. Place your arms at a slant, as if you were soaring through the air like a glider on a steep turn. Stretch your right arm forward as far as possible, while you simultaneously stretch your left arm backward. Imagine that someone is pulling on both of your arms as hard as they can, and you're feeling the strain in your shoulders. Reverse the procedure by stretching forward with your left arm and backward with your right. You'll know when you've done this exercise long enough because you'll feel a dull ache in your shoulder and upper arm muscles. Stop as soon as your body begins to feel tired.

Go back to your original starting position. Stand erect, with your hands on your hips and your feet slightly apart. Bend your body from the waist to the left, then bring it back upright. Then bend over to the right in the same manner. Stand erect and repeat this exercise, bending first to the right and then to the left.

From the starting position, bend forward, but keep your knees straight. Try to touch your palms to the floor a dozen times. Then try to slowly squat on your toes until you are in a sitting position. Stretch out your arms sideways for balance, as you squat. Then return your arms to your hips, as you rise. When doing this exercise, keep your back straight and your head up. Don't lean forward. Repeat this exercise ten or twelve times.

On a mat or a rug, lie flat on your back. Bend your knees and place your feet flat on the floor. With your hands clasped behind your neck, raise yourself into a sitting position, while keeping your knees bent. If you find this exercise easy to do, try it with your legs stretched out flat on the floor.

For your last warm-up exercise, lie flat on your stomach, with your legs straight out and your toes against the ground. With your palms flat against the mat, straighten your arms and raise your upper body. Keep your body as straight as possible while doing these push-ups, and try not to bend at the hips. Once this seems easy to do, try balancing on only one toe, while you lift your other leg. Always keep your stomach on the ground. Bring your leg down, while raising your body with your arm and shoulder muscles. Instructors of gymnastic exercise call these exercises "hyper-extended pushups." They readily admit that they're especially difficult for beginners to perform.

What have you accomplished during this pre-workout conditioning? You have limbered up your body muscles in order to make it easier for you to start acrobatics and gymnastics. You have accustomed your body to the same strains that every circus performer well knows. Whether you do these particular exercises or a similar series of calisthenics doesn't really matter. Just limber up and increase the number of exercises you do each day. They will soon become easier, and you will have less muscle strain. Eventually, you should work out no more than 15 to 20 minutes each day.

In a few weeks, you'll find that you're able to do three to four times as many warm-ups as you were able to do the first day, without any noticeable muscular strain. Then you'll be well on the way to becoming a circus acrobat.

2
Starting on Tumbling

DURING THE MIDDLE AGES, court jesters amused kings and nobles by doing somersaults, handstands, handsprings, and other acrobatic tricks. What they were really doing was tumbling.

Tumbling might be described as springing, twisting, turning, and rolling, according to set patterns—something children often do while playing. Basically, tumbling is merely training for more complicated tricks on gymnasium apparatus or perhaps for your act as a future Ringling Bros. and Barnum & Bailey Circus acrobat.

In most schools, group tumbling is done on mats stuffed with hair, felt, or plastic foam. The best way to learn tumbling is under the supervision of a professionally-trained instructor in a properly-equipped gymnasium. But there is no reason not to practice the following stunts on a living room rug,

5

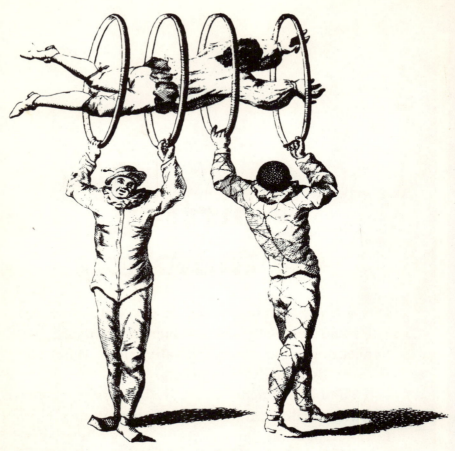

Clown-acrobats were the star performers in the early circus.
Circus World Museum, Baraboo, Wisconsin

on grass or even on a sandy beach. Just make sure there is plenty of open space all around you. Be very careful not to slip, twist or roll into a piece of furniture or any other indoor or outdoor obstacle.

To keep you safe from harm, practice what the professionals call "spotting". Tumble with a friend, whenever possible. One of you should always watch the other. The spotter should know exactly what you are going to do beforehand and which parts of the tumbling exercises are the most difficult for you. If you need a strong right arm to help you turn a somersault, your spotter can supply it until you can do the exercise without help. If you start to fall on your head, neck or back, your spotter can quickly help you land on your feet or knees or in a prone position.

Practicing tumbling techniques under the supervision of a spotter. *Nissen Corporation, Cedar Rapids, Iowa*

Tumbling practice at the children's Sailor Circus, Sarasota, Florida. *Charles R. Meyer*

Accidents don't just "happen;" they are usually caused by carelessness and overconfidence. Catching, lifting, pushing, or supporting a fellow performer during practice sessions are the best ways to prevent unnecessary injuries.

The important function of mats filled with hair, felt or plastic foam is to cushion your body against accidental falls, as well as to absorb most of the shock when you land. Most gymnasium mats are 4′ × 8′, 5′ × 10′, 6′ × 12′, 5′ × 30′, and 5′ × 40′.

Opposite: Learning balancing skills at the Ringling Bros. and Barnum & Bailey Clown College in Venice, Florida. *Charles R. Meyer*

If you have a mat or mattress to use as a landing field when tumbling, place it where you are most likely to hit the ground. If you're doing a handstand, place the mat where you think you'll land when you fall forward. If possible, double the thickness of the pads. Adjoining pads can separate if you land on them with a great deal of running momentum.

If you can't find any mats, be sure to use some soft substitute that will keep you from hurting yourself. Never, never tumble on concrete or hard wooden floors. Don't be overconfident, or forget that even the most expert acrobats and clowns, performing under the Big Top, bruise themselves when they fall too hard.

It would be nice if every tumbler could wear a colorful uniform, such as red-spangled tights, an embroidered top, and special shoes. Unfortunately, costumes can be expensive and also difficult to make at home. As a beginner, try wearing shorts and a tightfitting T-shirt. Sneakers are the best footgear. Don't wear any loose clothing that might catch or snag. And never wear any jewelry, such as rings, bracelets, necklaces or wristwatches. If you have long hair, tie it back so it can't fall forward and obstruct your vision in the middle of a somersault.

3
Acrobatic Rolls

FORWARD AND BACKWARD rolls are basic acrobatic stunts. They may seem difficult at first, but once you learn them, they will be as easy as riding a bicycle.

Lie flat on your stomach, with your toes against a mat. Place your palms on the floor beneath your shoulders, but underneath your body. In this position, push your body upward with your hands. Do several push-ups, lifting yourself until your arms are straight. Your body should be stiff rather than bent. Each time, lower your body until it is a few inches above the mat. Repeat the exercise.

The most common mistake beginners make when doing push-up exercises is arching their backs instead of keeping their bodies straight. Your spotter or instructor can help by placing one hand under your mid-section for support. This will be most helpful when you're a little tired or tempted to take short cuts.

Now let's try a tip-up.

Squat in a sitting position, with your rear end just above the floor. Place both hands flat against the mat, with your fingers forward and your knees braced against your elbows. Slowly lean forward. As your feet leave the floor, balance yourself on the palms of your hands and brace yourself with your elbows against the inside of your knees. If necessary, a spotter can help by holding your hips so you don't lean too far forward and fall over.

Now tilt backward until your feet are on the floor once again.

After you've mastered the tip-up, you can convert it to a forward roll in a "squat-to-stand" sequence. Assume the squat position once more, with your knees between your arms and your palms flat on the mat, on a line straight from your shoulders. Your fingers should be facing forward. Tuck your chin against your chest, and extend your legs backward with a slight push or jump until they are stretched out behind you. At the same time, roll forward, keeping your chin tightly tucked against your chest.

Your shoulders, back, and hips will in turn contact the mat, as you complete your first forward roll. When your feet touch the mat, fling your arms forward, and pull yourself into a normal standing position. Your spotter can help by kneeling close to you on one side of the mat, making sure that your

A spotter helps a performer start a forward roll. *Nissen Corporation, Cedar Rapids, Iowa*

chin remains tucked against your chest when you roll over. To make it easier to stand up at the end of your roll, make sure the front of your thighs are pressed closely against your stomach and the lower section of your chest.

Practice the "squat-to-stand" forward roll a few times until it becomes easy to do. You can then convert it to a "stand-to-stand" sequence by starting from a standing position and dropping into the squat position before you roll forward and rise to your feet.

Having trouble? Start from the squat position once again, and ask your spotter to put a hand behind your neck so that you can be guided through the entire maneuver. Some gymnastic instructors suggest that students who have difficulty in rolling should try to squat with their hands as close as possible to their feet. In addition, you might lie on your back, with your knees drawn tightly against your chest, and rock back and forth until you become accustomed to the rolling motion.

If you have any difficulty with the timing for this exercise, a spotter should kneel beside the mat and make sure that your head is tucked down against your chest when you begin the forward roll. Not before, not after—just as you begin the forward roll.

Here are a few variations on rolling exercises.

Instead of rising to your feet after the first forward roll, clasp your hands around your legs, just below your knees. Pull your body even tighter into a ball, or what gymnastic instructors call a "tuck." Roll forward again until you have accomplished a second, or even a third roll; then fling your arms forward and return to a standing position.

You have really done a basic, triple-forward

somersault. Trapeze artists in the Greatest Show On Earth® perform the same kind of somersault high in the air.

To do a "squat-to-stand" backward roll, start from the squatting position, with the palms of your hands against the ground and your knees between your arms. Lean forward very slightly, and then rock backward into your roll. As you sit on your backside, push both hands against the floor and roll onto your back. Place your hands, palms up, above your shoulders, with your fingers pointed backward in the direction of the roll. Keep your chin tucked against your chest. Now, roll over on the top of your head and back down onto your hands. Keep your knees tucked against your chest all the while. Finally, complete the exercise by pushing down with your hands and continuing the roll until you finish in the original squatting position. These movements must be done quickly so that you gain enough momentum to follow through with the roll.

Once you have thoroughly mastered the backward roll in the "squat-to-stand" sequence, try to do it in the "stand-to-stand" sequence, much as you did in the forward roll. You'll eventually be able to do two or three successive rolls.

You're now beginning to acquire the same kind of tumbling skills used by acrobats in the Ringling Bros. and Barnum & Bailey Circus.

If you have perfected all these tumbling rolls, try to combine several of them into one continuous exercise. Do a forward roll, stand up, and then do a backward roll. As you become more skilled, do two or three of each roll, and add other rolls, such as the shoulder roll. Blend them all into a single, circular exercise, as if you were performing in the center circus ring to the applause of the crowd.

4
Cartwheels and Somersaults

CIRCUS CLOWNS DELIGHT audiences with their acrobatic antics—suddenly turning cartwheels or doing handstands in the middle of the ring. If you'd like to perform these tricks, plus a number of variations, here's how.

To begin a cartwheel, first stand erect, with your legs about shoulder width apart, and your hands extended sideways at shoulder level. Raise your left leg if you're going to turn a cartwheel in that direction. Raise your right leg if you're headed the other way. Assuming you will be doing a cartwheel to the left, take a step and lean toward the left. Push your left foot into the mat. Kick your right foot over your head as you bend sideways. Your left hand should touch the ground first, followed immediately by your right hand. Your arms should be perfectly straight, and your head should be upright.

17

Circus clown-acrobats performed with elephants in the 1900s. *Circus World Museum, Baraboo, Wisconsin*

A cartwheel performed from the sitting position. *Nissen Corporation, Cedar Rapids, Iowa*

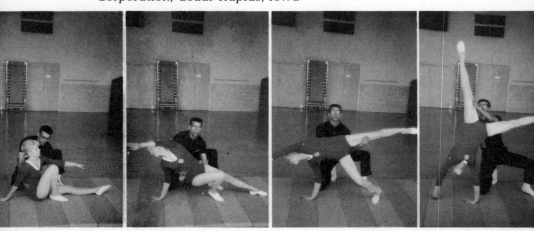

Spread your legs apart, as your body goes through the handstand position. Bend from your waist. Place first your left foot and then your right foot on the mat, as you start to return to the standing position. A spotter should see to it that your hand and foot positions form a straight line. If necessary, the spotter can stand behind you and support your left side with a hand as you flip over sideways. When you go into your handstand, the spotter should place a hand on your right side in order to guide you through the remainder of the cartwheel. A spotter could also find out whether the placement of your hands and feet on the mat form a straight line by chalking their positions before and during the cartwheel.

To do a cartwheel to the right, follow the same instructions, but reverse the order of your feet and hands.

Doing a round-off from a run. *Nissen Corporation, Cedar Rapids, Iowa*

If you find it difficult to learn the cartwheel, first try kicking up to a handstand and landing on the opposite foot from the last one to leave the mat. Once your hands and feet are coordinated, flip a bit harder. Then turn, instead of emerging in your original standing position. If a left cartwheel seems more difficult, practice going to the right until you become more expert.

Cartwheels are hard to do until you develop enough strength in your arms and shoulders to carry you through the basic maneuver. One-arm cartwheels are just a little bit harder. To do a one-arm cartwheel, first lean in the direction in which you want to go. Place your inside hand on the mat, and perform the cartwheel without making use of your other arm. At first you may find it necessary to lean slightly forward. But later on you'll discover that

20

you can keep your legs straight and your body rigid, and perform it correctly.

Let's carry your acrobatic gymnastics a bit further by doing a round-off. In this stunt you will finish your cartwheel in a position that will enable you to flip into a number of backward tumbling exercises. In effect, you'll be reversing the forward motion you gained by achieving backward momentum. Get a running start, and then skip with your right foot, while bringing your left foot forward. As you put your left foot on the ground, place your left hand on the mat, approximately two feet in front of you. Kick both feet overhead, one after the other, and place your right hand in front of you. Your hands and arms should pivot in the same direction in which your body is turning, or in a 90-degree angle. In the round-off, your body should be bent at

A round-off with a safety harness, followed by a back handspring. *Nissen Corporation, Cedar Rapids, Iowa*

The forward walkover is easy if you have an expert to spot trouble and to show you exactly what to do. *Nissen Corporation, Cedar Rapids, Iowa*

A back handspring from a round-off, assisted by a spotter.
Nissen Corporation, Cedar Rapids, Iowa

A step-out handspring is helped by the spotter's supporting hand pressing backward on the performer's shoulder. *Nissen Corporation, Cedar Rapids, Iowa*

the waist, and your legs should be more or less parallel to the floor. Quickly bring your feet down from your waist level to a standing position on the mat, while simultaneously pushing hard with your hands, arms, and shoulders. Land on the balls of your feet, facing the direction of your original approach, with your knees slightly bent and your body leaning backward. You are now ready to swing into another tumbling exercise.

The round-off is almost exactly the same tumbling trick as a cartwheel, but instead of facing sideways at the end of the maneuver, you will be adding another quarter turn before you land on both feet at once. When you become confident about doing a round-off, try combining it with a back roll. You'll be in a suitable position for the back roll after you complete the cartwheel-turn combination.

24

At this point, you are beginning to combine your various tumbling skills into a succession of continuing stunts of the kind performed by professional circus acrobats.

A trickier tumbling trick is a forward somersault in the air. To do a forward somersault, run forward and skip with your left foot, while bringing your right foot forward. Raise both arms over your head. Then plant both your feet on the mat. Stretch your arms upward as far as possible. Then bring them forward and downward, while you tuck your chin against your chest. Jump high into the air. (Professional tumblers usually continue the circular motion by grasping their shins with both of their hands, as they go into a tucked-chin position.) You should sail through the air like a ball, with your chest close to your knees and your heels against

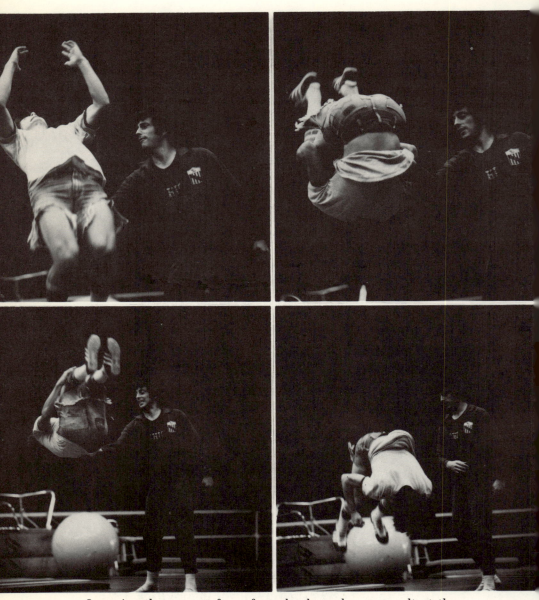

Learning the correct form for a backward somersault at the Clown College in Venice, Florida. *Charles R. Meyer*

Future circus performers learn tumbling and trapeze skills at the Sailor Circus in Sarasota, Florida. *Charles R. Meyer*

Clown students work out at the Clown College in Venice, Florida. *Charles R. Meyer*

your rear end. Once you have completed the somersault, straighten out and finish in a standing position.

A forward somersault in the air sounds simple, but it really isn't all that easy. A spotter can help you by standing at the starting, lift-off spot and placing one hand beneath your head or your shoulders to make sure you go into a tuck, or a ball position. The spotter's other hand might grasp your shoulder or upper arm to prevent you from spinning too far and losing control.

The best way to learn the forward somersault is with a tumbling belt, attached to two ropes, and the help of two spotters or with a safety harness and an instructor. Other accessories, such as a mini-tramp or a springboard trampoline, will enable you to gather enough height to make this stunt easier.

5
Partnerships and Comedy Routines

MANY OF THE basic tumbling exercises you have learned can delight an audience when humor is added to your routine. For example, there is a racing game, in which one tumbler lies flat on the floor on his or her stomach, and raises the body as if performing a push-up. The second team member picks up his or her legs and tucks them outside the hips, while the first tumbler walks alone on his or her hands. In gymnastics, this is usually called "the wheelbarrow."

In the circus, this race is often done as a clown routine. Two teams sometimes race each other. The clowns who are walking on their hands claim they are being forced to propel themselves in rapid circles around the ring. At the finish line, the non-performing clowns congratulate one another, as the other team members sprawl in the sawdust.

Forming a pyramid is always a crowd-pleasing act. *Ringling Bros. and Barnum & Bailey Circus*

One interesting variation of the racing game is to station clowns at frequent intervals along the race "track." The clowns then pass the hand-walker to each other, as if the hand-walker was the stick in a marathon relay.

Pyramid formations are other routines which

delight circus audiences. Pyramids are particularly effective when they are performed to appropriate music. Depending on the skill of the acrobats, pyramids can be built by adding more gymnasts horizontally, vertically or in a combination of both directions. Circus pyramids are often built many stories high by experienced acrobatic groups. Obviously, the higher the pyramid, the more unbalanced it will be, thus increasing the chances of its falling.

At the Ringling Bros. and Barnum & Bailey Circus training school for clowns in Florida, pupils often practice a routine called log rolling. Three clowns assume positions on their hands and knees in a straight line, about 15 inches apart. Jumping as high as possible by using both arms and legs, the clown on the left leaps over the clown in the middle and lands as close to the middle as possible. Meanwhile the middle clown rolls over and ends up on the left. As the gymnast from the left lands near the middle, he or she then rolls toward the right, while the performer on the right jumps to the middle and promptly rolls toward the left. The process is then repeated.

The action is continuous when log rolling is well done. The rolling motion is coordinated so that the three clowns perform gracefully and smoothly. When you first attempt log rolling, start very slowly and only speed up the tempo when the three other performers have mastered the routine.

You can duplicate a circus act if one acrobat

dresses in a clown's costume. Make sure the costume won't catch or snag during the act and cause an accident. The costume itself will provoke laughter, and if the clown has a funny personality, the audience will be even more delighted. Have several gymnasts line up and, one after the other, do cartwheels or somersaults over a rolled-up mat. Then have the clown at the end of the line wind up like a pitcher on a baseball mound, run toward the mat, stop, and then, at the last possible moment, gingerly step aside.

As a variation of this routine, have the clown do a series of cartwheels, switch into back rolls and a back somersault, and then stagger around the ring as though dizzy. The other acrobats should pretend to be highly indignant, as they argue with the clown. The clown should then strip off his outer shirt and reveal a T-shirt with an emblem, saying "Superman."

Another routine is to have a series of acrobats kneel in a row, while a good gymnast performs cartwheels on their backs. Then the clown tries to do the same thing, but merely runs awkwardly over the backs of the gymnasts.

Still another act starts with a loud argument between a clown and an acrobat. When the clown swings a broomstick at the acrobat's legs, the acrobat does a back flip, while the broom passes underneath. The clown is so impressed by this maneuver that he purposely starts an argument with another clown, tries the identical stunt, but gets painfully hit

A clown-tumbler flies through a hoop. *Charles R. Meyer*

Pio Nock, Europe's famous high-wire clown, bicycles the hard way. *Ringling Bros. and Barnum & Bailey Circus*

A pretty girl starts Pio Nock off on his high-wire act. *Ringling Bros. and Barnum & Bailey Circus*

on the shins. The clown laments loudly, then rushes around the ring looking for sympathy from the audience.

Clown-acrobat gags are endless in the circus, especially when trampolines, trapezes, high wires, and other special equipment are used. Try to invent your own routines, but make sure they are performed within sensible safety limits. Never take chances just to make the audience laugh.

6
Putting It All Together

AT RINGLING BROS. AND BARNUM & BAILEY Circus World in Florida, youngsters learn to walk on wires, while Ringling Bros. and Barnum & Bailey Circus professionals stand close by, ready to help the would-be acrobat in case of a misstep. There is no safety net, but the wire is strung only about six feet above the ground. At an actual show under the Big Top, the identical wire might be strung 60 to 100 feet high.

At youth circus performances, and in circus showmanship courses held in schools and other public gathering places all over the country, qualified adults teach children the basics of ground tumbling. The skills the children acquire may later be used for more complex routines. For instance, a ground tumbler or an acrobat who practices tumbling on a trapeze is known as a "famous flyer." If

Learning a complicated tumbling exercise with the aid of a safety harness helps the beginner to achieve a controlled landing. *Nissen Corporation, Cedar Rapids, Iowa*

the acrobats dress in outlandish costumes and ride bicycles across high wires, they then star as clowns. If a lady performs her acrobatic skills on a horse cantering around the center ring, she is then featured as a bareback rider.

Very often in the circus, acrobats perform many other acts besides those requiring acrobatic skills. Many of the acrobats in the Greatest Show on Earth® do much more than cartwheels and round-offs, yet they had to master fundamental acrobatic skills before going on to greater things!

With the help of an experienced instructor, you can learn more complicated movements, too. A safety harness, to which a rope is attached, will help. The rope, held by the instructor, keeps you from falling, when the teacher walks you through

exercises ordinarily done at a running pace. You are taught how to balance your weight, shift your center of gravity, and use the momentum gained from one exercise to bring you safely through another that might otherwise be dangerous.

Acrobatic routines are taught very gradually. Ideally, serious acrobatic training should begin when a boy or girl is between six and nine years old, but this is no reason why anyone can't begin at any age under twenty-five. Most of the comedians practicing acrobatics at the Clown College of the Ringling Bros. and Barnum & Bailey Circus in Florida range in age from approximately 18 to 25.

We have discussed basic tumbling skills at considerable length. Expert ground tumblers soon graduate to re-bound tumbling on a mini-tram-

Rebound tumbling on a
mini-trampoline spring-
board. *Charles R. Meyer*

The sky-high stunts of the Christos thrill circus audiences. *Ringling Bros. and Barnum & Bailey Circus*

Teeterboard tumblers and acrobats, the Bulgarian-born Boichanovis. *Ringling Bros. and Barnum & Bailey Circus*

The Malevoltis stage an acrobatic aerial show. *Ringling Bros. and Barnum & Bailey Circus.*

poline, a springboard of the type used under the Big Top, or a full-fledged trampoline of the sort found in school gymnasiums. But lessons for learning these skills are always given under competent instruction! Trampolines and similar equipment should never be used without the supervision of a professional teacher.

The dangers involved in trampolining, balancing in pyramids, vaulting on side or long horses, doing stunts on high or parallel bars, and rope climbing cannot be overemphasized. Never try experimenting with tumbling and acrobatic exercises lest you end up in a hospital with broken bones.

Needless to say, a baby learns to crawl before walking, and to walk before running. An acrobat must learn the fundamentals of ground tumbling before more complicated acrobatics and stunts on mechanical equipment can be mastered. There is no way that a boy or girl can become a circus star without going through this learning process, and there are no shortcuts. Perfecting acrobatic skills requires several years of constant practice.

Although many forms of entertainment, such as television and motion pictures, are available to almost everyone, nothing can take the place of the circus. Acrobatic acts are just as thrilling and dangerous as they were in the days when the Ringling Bros. first started with a tiny, one-ring traveling show.

There are fascinating circus museums in Baraboo, Wisconsin; Peru, Indiana; Somers, New York;

Carl Damann and his family were famous for their acrobatic daring and skills many years ago. *Circus World Museum, Baraboo, Wisconsin*

In 1904, the Florenz Troupe dressed in formal clothing for their acrobatic act. *Circus World Museum, Baraboo, Wisconsin*

and Sarasota, Florida. If you are fortunate enough to visit one, look at the displays of old posters featuring early circus acrobats. You'll discover that the exercises you've learned are the same as those used more than 100 years ago.

7
Acrobats from Rome to Ringling

IN ANCIENT ROME, rival politicians sponsored free chariot races and acrobatic spectacles of the "hair-raising" and "heart-stopping" kind we see today in the Ringling Bros. and Barnum & Bailey Circus. Circus audiences have always enjoyed watching acrobatic daredevils doing tricks, such as somersaulting over several elephants in a row. Sometimes motorcycling acrobats even vault their machines over obstacles.

When circus performer William Stokes wrote *The Vaulting Master* in 1652, he explained in detail how he had learned to leap over horses standing side-by-side, and to land in the saddle of the farthest horse's back. A former Dutch acrobat, Kees Kalmar, made his audiences gasp when he leaped through a hoop made of thirteen razor-sharp daggers. And an early American circus performer, Artressi, executed

43

Acrobats and dancers have many talents in common. *Ringling Bros. and Barnum & Bailey Circus*

The incomparable Ferco does a perfect split-leap from a tight-wire. *Ringling Bros. and Barnum & Bailey Circus*

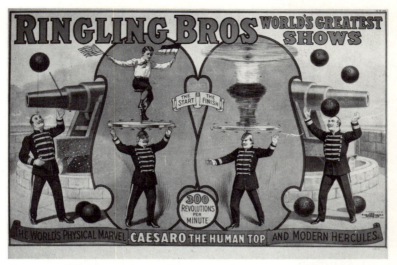

Caesaro, "the human top," was a circus sensation in 1912.
Circus World Museum, Baraboo, Wisconsin

a double somersault over four elephants topped by a pyramid of acrobats.

The dictionary defines acrobatics as "the evolutions of a person skilled in feats of agility and balance, but also one who walks on tiptoe." That definition suggests a close relationship between acrobats and dancers. The two have much in common.

In his book on the early English circus troupes, Anthony D. Hippisley Coxe writes that anyone who turns a somersault, swings on a trapeze or performs a difficult balancing act today is called an acrobat. But in the nineteenth century, things were quite different, according to Coxe. In the past, trapeze performers and other aerialists were called gymnasts, or aerial gymnasts, if they performed high in the air. They were called *parterre* (a French word, meaning on the earth), or "pattern" gymnasts, if they worked on the ground. Acrobats were known as tumblers until the times and the language changed.

John Bill Ricketts used a jump-up board to vault over ten horses as part of his American circus equestrian act in 1809. In 1817, when James West's English Circus company appeared in New York City, the management advertised an acrobatic clown who "... will leap over five horses and throw somersaults through a balloon of fire."

Popular nineteenth-century clowns, such as Dan Rice and Pete Conklin, often stood on the edge of the ring and sang a popular verse:

He floats through the air
With the greatest of ease,
The daring young man on the flying trapeze.

In the past, circus gymnasts raced onto spring-boards and soared into the air over all sorts of obstacles. Aerialists floated from one trapeze to another, as if they were birds gliding on the wind. Pretty girls in tights did somersaults, and landed bareback on horses cantering around center rings. All the world loved the early circus, which featured the stunts of agile acrobats. Today, that statement is just as true. Acrobats are the bricks with which much of the circus shows are built.

If you learn to be an acrobat through ground-

The Nelson Family were billed as premier acrobats in 1906
circus posters. *Circus World Museum, Baraboo, Wisconsin*

tumbling skills, as well as through gymnastics under
expert supervision and instruction, you may become
one of tomorrow's headliners in the Greatest Show
on Earth®.